Greetings,

The thought process behind creating this how to document on self-publishing is to help you make the most out of your decision to become a published author.

The success of your decision is totally up to you. Just as the saying goes, it is what you put into it that will determine the return.

To me writing is a passion. It is my purpose, my talent, my way of contributing back into this society. Once you can identify your area of writing whether it is in novels, mystery, romance, poetry, literature, education, nature the list can go on with no ending, the opportunities are endless.

The point is there are a wide variety of areas.

And if you want to explore more than one area, then it is your choice.

I say go for it!

Within this booklet you will gain the knowledge of:

- Recognizing that inner voice to write.
- Create and maintain your audience.
- Business Plan For Your Book
- Your Manuscript
- Book Cover Design
- Your Copy Rights
- Your ISBN
- Marketing & Distribution
- Book Signing

Congratulations on making the step towards being a published author.

So, now that you have arrived, let's get started on your path as a self-published author!

I recall when I mentioned the outcome of my first book people would say things like "you want to be a writer?"

The truth is I've been a writer, and so have you. We are just approaching the next level along the path.

I recently had a conversation with a writer that mentioned she is looking for her inspiration of a book. And wanted to know how to get started, my suggestion is that you find your focal point and build from there.

Once you can identify with your passion of a subject then you can begin to develop your writing style.

For example, I know my purpose is to inspire, encourage and motivate. Therefore, these are the things that I write about, whether it is through quotes, poetry or expounding on certain areas of our lives. The bottom line is that I am writing in a area that I have passion.

Here are some suggestions on introducing yourself into the world of writing and being published, developing your writing style, developing an audience.

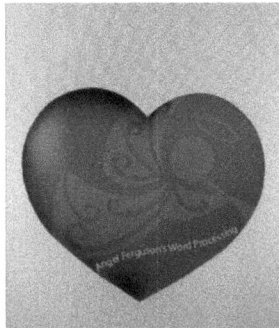

To begin with put your pen to paper or your fingers to the keyboard. And let the thoughts flow. Another suggestion would be to volunteer to write for a newsletter within the school's PTA, creating a blog, enter wring contest, etc.

When I first started writing, my sister and I would write different analogies to each other via mail. At the time, I wanted to develop a magazine, Hope & Truth Magazine.

I found myself wanting to write things that made me think of where I had been, where I was and where I wanted to go. I wanted to write things that caused one to really look beyond the surface of any situation.

That was 2005 and my passion has only grown stronger but with more direction and stability. I have a passion for what I love to do and that is being a publisher.

Now that you have found your voice, it's time to let the world listen!

Author Angel Ferguson

THE ROAD MAP TO SELF-PUBLISHING

THE DESIRE TO WRITE

FINDING YOUR ORIGINAL VOICE AS A WRITER

IDENTIFY YOUR AREA OF WRITING: FICTION, POETRY, SELF-HELP, INTEREST OR SPECIALITY

FACING AND GETTING OVER THE FEAR OF ALLOWING OTHERS TO READ YOUR WORK

STOP SECOND GUESSING YOURSELF! TAKE A STEP TOWARDS YOUR GOALS & DREAMS OF BECOMING A WRITER

BABY STEPS: LOCATING SOURCES TO PUBLISH ONLINE FOR FREE, START WRITING FOR UPCOMING OCCASSIONS

LET THE WRITING BEGAN! GATHER YOU'RE THOUGHTS & LET THE PEN TAKE OVER

CREATING A MANUSCRIPT FOR YOUR WORK

PROOF READING: GREAT FOR HIGH SCHOOL & COLLEGE KIDS, WITH COMPENSATION OF COURSE.

EDITING

DESIGNING A BOOK COVER; HERE IS AN IDEA, TAKE OUT YOUR CAMERA & TAKE YOUR OWN PICTURES.

HAVE AN ARTIST IN THE FAMILY ASK THEM TO DESIGN YOU A COVER. WITH COMPENSATION OF COURSE

DON'T FRET! YES YOU CAN AFFORD THIS!

SUBMITTING YOUR FINISHED MANUSCRIPT TO THE LOB:

IF YOU ARE THE SOLE WRITER, TO SUBMIT YOUR WORK ONLINE THE COST IS $ 55.00

IF IT IS A GROUP OF CONTRIBUTORS, THE COST IS $ 55.00

OBTAINING YOUR ISBN#

MARKETING: ADVERTISING: PROMOTION

UTILIZE ALL ONLINE RESOURCES TO DISCUSS YOUR BOOK!

ONLY YOU CAN DESCRIBE WHAT YOU WANT THE READERS TO FEEL AND THE IMPACT YOU WANT TO LEAVE, SO YOU CAN WRITE A PRESS RELEASE.

FINDING A DISTRIBUTION SITE FOR YOUR BOOK

UTILIZE AMAZON'S CREATE A SPACE!

IT'S FREE, YOU HAVE CONSTANT ASSISTANCE.

YOU WILL RECEIVE ASSISTANCE WITH PRICING YOUR BOOK,

ALONG WITH AMAZON'S SOURCES OF DISTRIBUTION

WANT TO HAVE YOUR BOOK CARRIED IN A BOOK STORE! YOU CAN DO THAT TOO!

ARE YOU INTERESTED IN SELLING COPIES OF YOUR BOOK? YOU MUST OBTAIN A LICENSE.

I have created a check list for your first project. No matter the size, planning is essential.

Identify your passion for writing.

Writing to me is?

_____

_____

_____

_____

Identify your area of interest..

I would like to
write:_____

_____

Start your writing journal.

Do some research of other authors that are writing the type of material you want to write.

Enter a writing class.

Write from what's in your soul

Surround yourself with those of the same interest.

Locate free webhosting sites that will allow you to sign up for free to submit your work.

Create a blog.

Friends and family are great proof readers.

Would I like to see my writing remain a hobby or a career?

Having a plan for your book is essential as with any other business adventure.

For me, I love to gather my thoughts about what I am writing before I can create the title. In my writing field I write food for thought, things that are meant to inspire whether through quotes or poetry. As in a business plan, you must know your target market. My market is for every area of ones life! Personal, Spiritual, Business & Family. I look at every area of growth.

Next, I can move forward with a plan to finance the publishing of a book, marketing, etc. Throughout this how to doc, I have given some cost effect ways to bring your dream of being a published author in-to a reality.

As a self-publisher remember, you have total control of how far you want your writing career to go.

What I have learned to do is to o prepare a plan of action per book and to revise the plan as needed.

A PLACE FOR NOTES:

One way to introduce yourself as a serious writer is to share your work with family & friends. While you are writing remain consistent with your tone, content and structure.

Start a writing journal, blog etc. There are countless free webhosting sites that are user friendly. Make sure to include all of your professional media networks as a source for more of your content. Here is a key, accept criticism. It will help develop you. And please don't be hard on yourself. As with anything practice makes perfect.

READ, EDIT, READ, EDIT, READ & EDIT AGAIN!

Editing is essential. Our eyes and fingers often play tricks on us. Our thought process might say one thing but we will type another. So what I have learned to do is to get an editor. Not just one but two. We will discuss the budget for this later. I have found myself in a position of pressing the publish button only to find errors. So I must remind myself to relax, and not rush. And here is the most import thing to remember throughout your life and career, no method is perfect. The more we write, the more we understand our talents. The more we write the more we learn of our patterns, we notice what works and what does not work. But lose the notion that in order for you to do this you have to be perfect.

There are times when I can read over a sentence several times and not catch the missing grammar. My spell check is on but what about the grammar?

Here is where your proof reader comes in handy. One that is objective and not just around for the money as all components to a book are important. Not just the author!

Another thing I have learned is that I need to give my proof reader and editor a time frame. A dead line so to speak. I, like a publishing company have given myself deadlines, goals in which I need a book ready for the Library of Congress, AMAZON'S CREATESPACE, promotion, etc.

Here's the thing when you receive that proof in the mail, give it over to an editor. I say this because we will get excited because our work is in actual print and we will miss a lot of things. One can never assume our eyes will catch everything, it will not.

A PLACE FOR NOTES:

_____

_____

_____

_____

_____

_____

_____

_____

_____

Let's be realistic. It takes some time to write a book. Below, I have created some highlights that we all should consider when gathering our team for the job at hand.

First of all, put yourself in the hiring manager's position. You are about to interview, learn of, recognize strengths and weaknesses in order to accomplish your goal.

Below is a list of the positions you need to fill:

Writer: YOU

Editor: make sure this person is a reliable source. Someone who will not share your work, take your work or one that will actually do the work.

Proofreader: the same applies to the notes above.

Graphic Artist: later we will discuss taking your own pictures. But of course if you are able to hire a graphic artist at a reasonable price, I say go for it. I am fortunate to have a son that is currently studying graphic arts. We have worked out his price. I have accomplished two goals here. I have my artwork being done and I am helping to assist someone else establish a career. I am able to utilize his talents in other areas of my business. When I create inspirational magnets, promotional signs, etc. he creates the art.

Publisher: When being cost effective, try Amazon. You can do the process or if it is too complicated, there is a small fee to do the uploading for you. But keep in mind, editing & proofing is not apart of that service. The service is just to have your book uploaded and the cover fitted.

We will discuss some advertising and promotion avenues later for you to take.

A PLACE FOR NOTES:

_____

_____

_____

_____

_____

_____

_____

_____

_____

_____

CREATING A MANUSCRIPT FOR YOUR WORK

DESIGNING A BOOK COVER; HERE IS AN IDEA, TAKE OUT YOUR CAMERA & TAKE YOUR OWN PICTURES.

HAVE AN ARTIST IN THE FAMILY ASK THEM TO DESIGN YOU A COVER.

WITH COMPENSATION OF COURSE

DON'T FRET! YES YOU CAN AFFORD THIS!

PROOF READING: GREAT FOR HIGH SCHOOL & COLLEGE KIDS, WITH COMPENSATION OF COURSE.

EDITING

Because we are in a world where having your copy rights for your work is essential, I believe in making sure that I own the rights to all of my work from beginning to end. When I want to design a cover, I take out my camera. I am also fortunate enough to have a son that is into commercial arts. He has taken over the job of designing my book covers, (for a fee of course).

There is another reason why I take out my camera, there is too much of the same on the internet. There are many quotes but the same back drop. I say appreciate your individual voice! There is nothing compared to having a vision to go along with the spoken words. In this retrospect, you are being covered legally. When the time comes to submit your work to the Library of Congress for your copy rights, feel free to enter your name or your designer in the appropriate fields.

Please keep in my mind that as you are creating your own back drops and book covers, you are making a way for your brand. You are establishing your own style. When your collection of work has been presented, your brand will stand out.

When considering taking out your camera, relax. Take out your phone first. There were times that I would use the camera on my phone until I could purchase a camera. Don't worry about all the extras on the side of your pictures, simply crop the image. With the proper software you can make your image into an award winning cover.

A PLACE FOR NOTES:

_____

_____

_____

_____

_____

_____

_____

_____

_____

SUBMITTING YOUR FINISHED MANUSCRIPT TO THE LOB:

IF YOU ARE THE SOLE WRITER, TO SUBMIT YOUR WORK ONLINE THE COST IS $ 55.00

IF IT IS A GROUP OF CONTRIBUTORS, THE COST IS $ 55.00

OBTAINING YOUR ISBN#

Long after the pleasure of collecting your ideas, doing some research, writing notes and bring it all together into a manuscript it's time to set a date to submit your work to the Library of Congress. I encourage you to have more than yourself as a proof reader. Have the final copy of the manuscript edited again. You can never be too sure. This is a learning experience. Also, if you have any family that has the free time to lend a hand in proofing your work that would be great. Make sure to spell check and to do a grammar check on your work. Here is a key factor, do not take the noted corrections personal. You want to present your best and that is the purpose of the proof reader and the editor.

If you are going to go for a professional proof reader, shop around.

Consider the services they offer.

What I have learned is that proofing and editing are two different things.

To me common sense would be to edit as I proof.

When submitting your completed manuscript to the Library of Congress, please pay attention that your file has been uploaded fully. Take the initiative to contact them. There are two options for submitting your work: E-File or Mail In-Paper Form. Currently the lead time for E-Filing your manuscript is up to 8 months and the paper form is 13 months. I encourage all to print the forms from the website to make sure that you have all of the information readily available before submitting online.

Below you will see a sample outline of the FORM X from the Library of Congress. This form is available online for your convenience.

1. TITLE OF THIS WORK_____

(If the work you are submitting has been revised and the title has been changed, there is a space for that also)

PREVIOUS OR ALTERNATIVE TITLES_____

PUBLICATION AS A CONTRIBUTION (If this work was published to a periodical, serial, or a collection, give this information about the collective work in which the contribution appeared)

2. NAME OF THE AUTHOR_____

DATE OF BIRTH OR IF THE AUTHOR HAS DECESASED

NATURE OF AUTHORSHIP: Briefly describe the nature of the material created by the author in which one is claiming a copyright.

Here are some very important questions on the form: Was the contribution to the work "work for hire?

AUTHOR'S NATIONALITY OR DMICLE (NAAME OF COUNTRY)

(IF THERE IS MORE THAN ONE AUTHOR, THERE IS A SPACE FOR EACH INDIVUALS INFORMATION)

3. YEAR IN WHICH THIS WORK WAS COMPLETED. (Once again if this work has been previously published, please provide the original date of completion.

4. COPYRIGHT CLAIMANT (S)_____

Please provide all names and address for those that have a towards this book, even if it is the same name as the author.

TRANSFER :_____

If the work has been transferred to a new party of ownership, then that

documentation is needed as well.

5. FOR PREVIOUS REGISTRATION: Has this registration or an earlier version been submitted to the Copyright Office?

If the answer is yes, why are you a submitting a new registration?

6. FEES. I make my payments online per submission. There is of course an option to set up an account in which payments are made from within the Copyright Office.

7. CORRESPONDENCE:_____

Give the name and address of where all correspondence for this application should go to.

As noted previously it does take some time to receive your certified copy of the copyright notice in the mail but in my experience patience is going to become your best friend.

A PLACE FOR NOTES:

_____

_____

_____

_____

_____

_____

_____

_____

_____

OBTAINING YOUR ISBN

Obtaining your ISBN, the International Standard Book Number. An ISBN is assigned to each edition and variation (except re-printings) of a book. For example, an e-book, a paperback, and a hardcover edition of the same book would each have a different ISBN

I know that if this is your first time writing a publishing a book then you will not know up front what an ISBN is and the purpose of the ISBN. After some research, I have found some answers to a lot of the questions that where before me.

The letters ISBN stand for: The International Standard Book Number (ISBN).

This a unique 13 digit number that identifies your book and it's book like products that have been published internationally. The purpose of is to establish and identify one title or edition of a title from one specific publisher and is unique to that edition, this allows a more efficient process for marketing for all those that intend to sell or carry your products.

ISBN issuance is country-specific, in that ISBNs are issued by the ISBN registration agency that is responsible for that country or territory regardless of the publication language. I used the source of ISBN.ORG. There are of course countless resources available on the internet. The process is simple, once you find the service to fit your budget and your needs.

The process to obtain the ISBN varies. My information was processed online and the number was readily available.

Please keep in mind that just because you have obtained your ISBN it does not apart of marketing your book. This number simply identifies your book.

Once issued, an ISBN is for that product alone and there is no transferring of this number to another title.

If you intend on writing a series then you can obtain both an ISBN & a ISSN.

Both numbering systems are used for books in a series and with annuals or biennials. The ISBN identifies the individual book in a series or a specific year for an annual or biennial. The ISSN identifies the ongoing series, or the ongoing annual or biennial serial. If a publication has both, each should be printed on the copyright page.

There are two places in which you can place your ISBN. Either on the copy right page or if there is no barcode then on the back cover is fine. Please note a barcode and an ISBN are two different numbers. The barcode tracks (scans) the sales of the product, yet it is assigned individually as well.

In short, if you have written the book and are not ready to place the book in the market for sale, there is no need for an ISBN or a barcode.

A PLACE FOR NOTES:

_____

_____

_____

_____

_____

_____

_____

_____

_____

MARKETING: ADVERTISING: PROMOTION

UTILIZE ALL ONLINE RESOURCES TO DISCUSS YOUR BOOK!

ONLY YOU CAN DESCRIPE WHAT YOU WANT THE READERS TO FEEL

AND THE IMPACT YOU WANT TO LEAVE,

SO YOU CAN WRITE A PRESS RELEASE.

As I am deep into this world of self-publishing, marketing has to begin along with the concept of your material. Developing a voice among a receptive audience is imperative in order to survive. The voice begins as a whisper and it will depend on how well you speak and interact which will determine if your voice has a chance to develop.

Marketing is sharing your content. Marketing is also listening. During this process, I have learned to read, listen and understand the basic principles of presenting my published books to book stores and the library system with ease.

The process is not as cumbersome as some will have us to believe. So as you are entering this process and not sure of which road to take, first learn of the establishment that you would like to place your book.

Learn of their process and procedures. Make an initial phone call so that they are familiar with your name. Include your established networking groups that you are active in. Write a presentation letter of your published book with a copy and allow time for the manager to review your book.

The approval for them to sell your book will come.

As always, write that letter with the same confidence that you had when writing your book.

A PLACE FOR NOTES:

_____

_____

_____

_____

_____

_____

_____

_____

_____

_____

FINDING A DISTRIBUTION SITE FOR YOUR BOOK

UTILIZE YOUR FACEBOOK AND ALL OF YOUR POSITIVE SOCIAL MEDIA OUTLETS.

PLEASE UTILIZE AN ESTABLISHED OUTLET IN WHICH YOUR NAME HAS BEEN ESTABLISHED.

IF YOU DO NOT HAVE A WEBSITE, HERE IS THE TIME TO OBTAIN ONE!

UTILIZE AMAZON'S CREATE A SPACE!

IT'S FREE, YOU HAVE CONSTANT ASSISTANCE.

YOU WILL RECEIVE ASSISTANCE WITH PRICING YOUR BOOK, ALONG WITH AMAZON'S SOURCES OF DISTRIBUTION

Here are some avenues that I have come upon. I recently wanted to branch out a little more as to where my books are found. So I checked out a major retail chain. I took the same steps as approaching a small book store. This process is more time consuming.

When submitting your book, please make sure you have all of the shipping dimensions. There is an option of having the company send you a order acknowledgement once a customer makes a purchase and you therefore ship the book to the customer or you can send them some of your books and they will ship the product for you.

In reality distribution and advertising will go hand in hand at this point. Your book will appear on their website. They in turn will utilize all of the avenues that one can find your book for purchase.

WANT TO HAVE YOUR BOOK CARRIED IN A BOOK STORE! YOU CAN DO THAT TOO!

ARE YOU INTERESTED IN SELLING COPIES OF YOUR BOOK? YOU MUST OBTAIN A LICENSE.

During the journey of writing, publishing and finding distribution, I relied on a lot of information located through businesses that actually provide the services I needed. I looked over what they offered and did the ground work myself. For instance, I wanted to have my first book in a local book store, I took the following steps: contacted the book store to learn if they were accepting new books and their policy. Next I researched how to write a letter of distribution. I detailed the competitive pricing, a proposal of a percentage, included a copy of the book and made my presentation.

Keep in mind that presentation is everything. Make sure you create your document the same way as if a big publishing company would. In fact you are a publishing company., a one person publishing company! Make sure that your letter is tailored to the individual store. I say this because you want that particular store to feel that you are reaching out to only them., they are an individual not a group unless of course you are writing to WALMART.

A PLACE FOR NOTES:

_____

_____

_____

_____

_____

_____

_____

_____

_____

And of course there are the large chains that require an actual application. Don't fret, this is achievable as well. Some large book chains require at least 2 finished copies of your book, some details about the book , their offered percentages, etc. The time in which you receive a response is long but there are countless other local book stores that you have access to in your area.

What I have come across is that some book stores have a special section for self-publishers. There is sometimes a small membership fee, but it is worth it. You are doing what publishing companies would do. Apart of your fees to the publishing company would go towards locating distribution for your book. Here is a bonus when dealing with local book stores, you are invited to do a book signing! This is another job you have accomplished all on your own.

Yes, the ground work is a lot but it is apart of the reward of being a self-publisher. Who knows there might come a time that you will forward all of these tasks to a publishing company but at least you will know just what goes into the process.

Here is another great source, AMAZON'S CREATESPACE.

Once your book has gone through the checks and balance, your book will be listed on their affiliate sites. To me the bigger part of letting others know that your book is out their relies on you. When presenting your book to anyone, give the purpose of your book. Give a little story behind what inspired the book. Draw the attention, keep it so that there is interest in purchasing not only this book but your future books as well. Their system is great, they keep track of your sales, there is also an option to have your book apart of KINDLE. That's another source for sales of your book.

Finally, there is the exposure of selling copies of your book yourself. There are many opportunities for you to do this. Apart of being with AMAZON's CREASPACE, that you can order copies of your book at whole sale. This is also something that the publishing company offers.

The copies of your book at your book launch, you can make sure those that did not preorder have a chance right then and their to purchase. Of course you must retain a retail license in order to sell your book. Ensure that you have either purchased your ISBN or, CREATESPACE will provide you with one! Yes, I know, awesome.

Here is another resource, there are countless online book sites that you can add your title and book cover too. Some are for free and some carry a small charge. I recommend that you check out what's on FACE-BOOK,LINKEDIN and other social media groups. Within these resources you can connect with other writers and gain some very helpful knowledge!

RESOURCES:

LIBRARY OF CONGRESS (US.COPYRIGHT.GOV)

If you would like to mail in your manuscript along with the payment, the mailing address is

The Library of Congress
101 Independence Ave, SE
Washington, DC 20540

OBTAINING YOUR ISBN (ISBN.ORG)
U.S. ISBN Agency
630 Central Avenue
New Providence, NJ 07974
Fax: 908-219-0188

Your County Business Tax Division

Your County Library

AMAZON CREATE SPACE: CreateSpace.com. This site is great. You can sign up for free, create your titles, participate in their online forums and have access to their online tools.

Here is a bonus, if you are unable to purchase an ISBN number CRE-ATESPACE can assign you one for free. You can also pay $ 10.00 to have your name listed as the publisher.

A PLACE FOR NOTES:

I sincerely hope that you have found the information within this how to doc of self-publishing very helpful. There is an understanding that if we could have a good set of resources in one setting then it does make the process easier. Are we claiming to know everything? NO. As with technology, information changes daily. It is up to each person to stay in tuned and up to date.

The information being presented are my experiences. As I am still experiencing.

During the process of writing, I have learned to keep a journey of each new thing I have learned. This is how we develop and grow and walking in knowledge having confidence when we speak on a subject.

During my journey of writing, I've expanded to an online magazine and a monthly newsletter. I love to write. I love to inspire and motivate. I love to share. This is my passion. This is my gift, and I am learning daily how to make changes so that what I love and have a passion for does not appear to be as work but something that is as natural as walking.

As I end each Morning Inspiration, stay encouraged, encouraging others along the way.

Sincerely,

Angel Ferguson

Publisher

www.ingramcontent.com/pod-product-compliance
Lightning Source LLC
Chambersburg PA
CBHW071344290326
41933CB00040B/2314